· Prep25 MIN

## Ingredients

1 pound bulk Italian sausage

1 medium onion, chopped (1/2 cup)

3 cans (15 ounces each) Italian-style tomato sauce

2 teaspoons dried basil leaves

1/2 teaspoon salt

2 cups shredded mozzarella cheese (8 ounces)

1 container (15 ounces) part-skim ricotta cheese

1 cup grated Parmesan cheese

15 uncooked lasagna noodles

## Steps

· 1

Cook sausage and onion in 10-inch skillet over medium heat 6 to 8 minutes, stirring occasionally, until sausage is no longer pink; drain. Stir in tomato sauce, basil and salt.

- 2

Mix 1 cup of the mozzarella cheese and the ricotta and Parmesan cheeses. (Refrigerate remaining mozzarella cheese while lasagna cooks.)

- 3

Spoon one-fourth of the sausage mixture into 6-quart slow cooker; top with 5 noodles, broken into pieces to fit. Spread with half of the cheese mixture and one-fourth of the sausage mixture. Top with 5 noodles, remaining cheese mixture and one-fourth of the sausage mixture. Top with remaining 5 noodles and remaining sausage mixture.

- 4

Cover and cook on Low heat setting 4 to 6 hours or until noodles are tender.

- 5

Sprinkle top of lasagna with remaining 1 cup mozzarella cheese. Cover and let stand about 10 minutes or until cheese is melted. Cut into pieces.

# *Slow-Cooker Spinach-Mushroom Tortellini*

## Ingredients

1 package (8 oz) white button mushrooms, thinly sliced

1 cup thinly sliced yellow onions

4 tablespoons butter, melted

2 tablespoons soy sauce

1/2 teaspoon salt

1/2 teaspoon pepper

2 cups Progresso™ Broth Vegetable(from 32-oz carton)

1 package (20 oz) refrigerated cheese-filled tortellini

1 package (8 oz) cream cheese, softened and cubed

3 cups baby spinach leaves, lightly packed

1/2 cup shredded Parmesan cheese (2 oz)

1/4 cup shredded fresh basil leaves

## Steps

- 1

Spray 4 1/2- to 5-quart slow cooker with cooking spray. Mix mushrooms, onions, melted butter, soy sauce, salt and pepper in cooker. Pour vegetable broth over vegetable mixture.

- 2

Cover; cook on Low heat setting 7 to 8 hours or until vegetables are very tender and browned.

- 3

Stir in tortellini and cream cheese. Cover; cook on Low heat setting 15 minutes. Cook and stir 14 to 16 minutes longer or until tortellini are tender. Stir in spinach. Let stand 5 minutes. Top with Parmesan cheese and basil.

# Slow-Cooker Bacon-Ranch Chicken and Pasta

- Prep 10 MIN

## Ingredients

1 lb chicken breasts

6 slices bacon, cooked and diced

2 to 3 cloves garlic, finely chopped

1 package (1 oz) ranch dressing and seasoning mix

1 can (10.75 oz) condensed cream of chicken soup

1 cup sour cream

1/2 teaspoon pepper

1/2 cup water

8 oz spaghetti, cooked

## Steps

- 1

Spray 4-quart slow cooker with cooking spray; place chicken breasts in cooker.

- 2

In medium bowl, mix remaining ingredients except spaghetti. Pour over top of chicken.

- 3

Cover; cook on Low heat setting 6 hours or on High heat setting 3 to 4 hours.

- 4

When about 15 minutes are left, cook and drain spaghetti as directed on package.

- 5

Just before serving, shred chicken with 2 forks, and toss creamy chicken mixture with cooked spaghetti.

## Slow-Cooker Cheesy Italian Tortellini

## Ingredients

1/2 lb lean (at least 80%) ground beef

1/2 lb bulk Italian sausage

1 container (15 oz) refrigerated marinara sauce

1 cup sliced fresh mushrooms

1 can (14.5 oz) diced tomatoes with Italian herbs, undrained

1 package (9 oz) refrigerated cheese-filled tortellini

1 cup shredded mozzarella cheese or pizza cheese blend (4 oz)

## Steps

- 1

In 10-inch skillet, cook beef and sausage over medium-high heat 5 to 7 minutes, stirring occasionally, until brown; drain.

- 2

Spray inside of 4- to 5-quart slow cooker with cooking spray. Mix beef mixture, marinara sauce, mushrooms and tomatoes in cooker.

- 3

Cover; cook on Low heat setting 7 to 8 hours.

- 4

Stir in tortellini; sprinkle with cheese. Cover; cook on Low heat setting about 15 minutes longer or until tortellini are tender.

# Slow-Cooker Meaty Italian Spaghetti Sauce

- Prep15 MIN

## Ingredients

2 lb bulk Italian pork sausage or ground beef

2 large onions, chopped (2 cups)

2 cups sliced fresh mushrooms (6 oz)

3 cloves garlic, finely chopped

1 can (28 oz) Muir Glen™ organic diced tomatoes, undrained

2 cans (15 oz each) tomato sauce

1 can (6 oz) tomato paste

1 tablespoon dried basil leaves

1 teaspoon dried oregano leaves

1 tablespoon sugar

1/2 teaspoon salt

1/2 teaspoon pepper

1/2 teaspoon crushed red pepper flakes

## Steps

- 1

Spray 5-quart slow cooker with cooking spray. In 12-inch skillet, cook sausage, onions, mushrooms and garlic over medium heat about 10 minutes, stirring occasionally, until sausage is no longer pink; drain.

- 2

Spoon sausage mixture into cooker.

- 3

Stir in remaining ingredients.

- 4

Cover; cook on Low heat setting 8 to 9 hours.

# *Slow-Cooker Italian Sausages and Peppers with Rotini*

- 

Prep15 MIN

## Ingredients

Reynolds™ Slow Cooker Liners

1 package (19.5 oz) turkey Italian sausages, cut into 1-inch pieces

1 cup finely chopped sweet onion

4 cloves garlic, finely chopped (2 teaspoons)

2 medium yellow bell peppers, cut into 1/2-inch pieces

2 medium red bell peppers, cut into 1/2-inch pieces

1 jar (26 oz) tomato pasta sauce

4 1/2 cups uncooked rotini pasta (12 oz)

6 tablespoons shredded Parmesan cheese

## Steps

- 1

Place Reynolds™ Slow Cooker Liners inside a 5- to 6 1/2 -qt slow cooker bowl. Make sure that liner fits snugly against the bottom and sides of bowl and pull the top of the liner over rim of bowl. In cooker liner, mix all ingredients except pasta and cheese.

- 2

Cover; cook on Low heat setting 6 to 8 hours.

- 3

Cook and drain pasta as directed on package. Serve sausage mixture over pasta; sprinkle with Parmesan cheese.

# SLOW-COOKER PASTA RECIPES READY IN UNDER 6 HOURS

## Creamy Tomato Slow-Cooker Chicken

## Ingredients

4 boneless skinless chicken breasts (about 1 1/4 lb)

2 cloves garlic, finely chopped

1 teaspoon dried basil leaves

1/2 teaspoon dried oregano leaves

1/4 teaspoon pepper

1 jar (15 oz) Alfredo sauce

1 can (14.5 oz) Muir Glen™ organic fire roasted petite diced tomatoes, drained

1 can (8 oz) Muir Glen™ organic tomato sauce

1 box (12 oz) uncooked pasta (such as penne or mostaccioli)

2 tablespoons cornstarch

2 tablespoons water

1/2 cup shredded Italian cheese blend (2 oz), if desired

## Steps

• 1

Spray 3- to 4-quart slow cooker with cooking spray. Arrange chicken in bottom of slow cooker. Top with garlic, basil, oregano and pepper.

- 2

In separate bowl, stir together Alfredo sauce, tomatoes and tomato sauce until well combined. Pour mixture over chicken.

- 3

Cover; cook on Low heat setting 5 to 6 hours.

- 4

Ten to 15 minutes before serving time, cook pasta as directed on package. In small bowl, stir together cornstarch and water; stir into mixture in slow cooker. Increase heat setting to High; cook uncovered 5 to 10 minutes longer.

- 5

Serve chicken with pasta; top with cheese.

# *Slow-Cooker Chicken Alfredo Tortellini*

- 

Prep5 MIN

## Ingredients

1 1/2 lb boneless skinless chicken breast

Salt and pepper to taste

2 cups sliced fresh mushrooms

1/2 cup Progresso™ chicken broth (from 32-oz carton)

3 cups Alfredo pasta sauce

2 or 3 cloves garlic, finely chopped

1 package (19 oz) refrigerated cheese tortellini

3 cups baby spinach

Grated Parmesan cheese

## Steps

- 1

Spray 6-quart slow cooker with cooking spray. Place chicken breast in slow cooker. Season with salt and pepper. Top with mushrooms, then chicken broth.

- 2

In medium bowl, mix Alfredo sauce and garlic. Pour over chicken and mushrooms. Cover; cook on Low heat setting 5 hours.

- 3

Shred chicken with 2 forks. Add cheese tortellini and spinach to slow cooker; stir. Cover; cook about 10 minutes or until pasta is cooked.

- 4

Top servings with Parmesan cheese, and enjoy.

# *Slow-Cooker Red Pepper-Spinach Lasagna*

## Ingredients

1 jar (26 to 28 oz) tomato pasta sauce

2 red bell peppers, chopped

1 medium onion, chopped (1/2 cup)

2 boxes (9 oz each) frozen chopped spinach, thawed, squeezed to drain

1 can (8 oz) Muir Glen™ organic tomato sauce

9 uncooked lasagna noodles

1 jar (16 oz) Alfredo pasta sauce

15 slices (1 oz each) provolone cheese

1/4 cup grated Parmesan cheese

## Steps

• 1

Spray 5- to 6-quart slow cooker with cooking spray. Spread 3/4 cup of the tomato pasta sauce in bottom of slow cooker.

• 2

In large bowl, mix bell peppers, onion and spinach; stir in remaining tomato pasta sauce and the tomato sauce.

- 3

Layer 3 lasagna noodles, broken into pieces to fit, over sauce in slow cooker. Top with one-third of the Alfredo sauce (about 1/2 cup), spreading to cover noodles completely. Top with 5 of the cheese slices, overlapping if necessary. Top with one-third of the vegetable mixture (about 2 cups), spreading evenly. Repeat layers twice. Sprinkle Parmesan cheese over top.

- 4

Cover; cook on Low heat setting 5 to 6 hours.

# *Skinny Slow-Cooker Spinach Lasagna*

- Prep30 MIN

## Ingredients

1 jar (25.5 oz) Muir Glen™ organic tomato basil pasta sauce

1 can (14.5 oz) Muir Glen™ organic fire roasted crushed or diced tomatoes, undrained

1/4 teaspoon crushed red pepper, if desired

1 yellow bell pepper, coarsely chopped

1 zucchini, halved and thinly sliced

9 uncooked lasagna noodles

1 1/4 cups light ricotta cheese

1 1/2 cups shredded part-skim mozzarella cheese (6 oz)

4 cups coarsely chopped fresh baby spinach (4 oz)

## Steps

- 1

Spray 5- to 6-quart slow cooker with cooking spray. In medium bowl, mix pasta sauce, tomatoes, crushed red pepper, bell pepper and zucchini. Spread 1 cup tomato mixture in bottom of slow cooker.

- 2

Layer 3 lasagna noodles, broken into pieces to fit, over sauce in slow cooker. Spread half of the ricotta cheese over noodles; sprinkle with 1/4 cup of the mozzarella cheese and half of the spinach. Top with one-third of the tomato sauce mixture (about 1 1/2 cups). Repeat layering of noodles, cheeses and spinach. Top with remaining 3 noodles and sauce. Save remaining 1 cup mozzarella cheese in refrigerator.

- 3

Cover; cook on Low heat setting 4 to 5 hours or until noodles are tender and cooked through. Sprinkle with reserved mozzarella; cover and let stand 10 minutes to melt cheese.

# Slow-Cooker Cheesy Ravioli Casserole (Crowd Size)

## Ingredients

1 tablespoon olive or vegetable oil

1 medium onion, chopped (1/2 cup)

1 large clove garlic, finely chopped

1 can (26 ounces) four cheese-flavored spaghetti sauce

1 can (15 ounces) tomato sauce

1 teaspoon Italian seasoning

2 packages (25 ounces each) frozen beef-filled ravioli

2 cups shredded mozzarella cheese (8 ounces)

1/4 cup chopped fresh parsley

## Steps

- 1

In 10-inch skillet, heat oil over medium heat. Cook onion and garlic in oil about 4 minutes, stirring occasionally, until onion is tender. Stir in spaghetti sauce, tomato sauce and Italian seasoning.

- 2

Place 1 cup of the sauce mixture in bottom of 5- to 6-quart slow cooker. Add 1 package frozen ravioli; top with 1 cup of the cheese. Top with remaining package of ravioli; top with remaining 1 cup cheese. Pour remaining sauce mixture over top.

- 3

Cover and cook on low heat setting 5 to 7 hours or until ravioli are tender. Sprinkle with parsley.

# *Slow-Cooker Chicken Parmesan with Penne Pasta*

- Prep15 MIN

## Ingredients

1 egg

1/3 cup Progresso™ plain bread crumbs

1/3 cup shredded Parmesan cheese

1/2 teaspoon Italian seasoning

1/4 teaspoon salt

1/4 teaspoon pepper

4 boneless skinless chicken breasts (about 1 1/4 lb)

1 jar (26 oz) tomato pasta sauce

1/2 cup shredded Italian cheese blend (2 oz)

2 2/3 cups uncooked penne pasta (8 oz)

## Steps

- 1

Spray 2- to 3-quart slow cooker with cooking spray.

- 2

In small shallow bowl, beat egg until foamy. In separate shallow bowl, mix bread crumbs, Parmesan cheese, Italian seasoning, salt and pepper. Dip chicken into egg, then coat evenly with bread crumb mixture; place in cooker. Spread pasta sauce evenly over chicken.

- 3

Cover; cook on Low heat setting 5 to 6 hours.

- 4

Sprinkle Italian cheese blend over top. Cover; cook on Low heat setting 10 minutes longer. Meanwhile, cook and drain pasta as directed on package. Serve chicken with pasta.

# SLOW-COOKER PASTA RECIPES READY IN UNDER 5 HOURS

## Slow-Cooker Cheesy Chicken Enchilada Pasta

## Ingredients

1 can (10 oz) Old El Paso™ mild enchilada sauce

1 package (0.85 oz) Old El Paso™ chicken taco seasoning mix

1 package (20 oz) boneless skinless chicken thighs

1/2 cup chopped onion

3 cloves garlic, finely chopped

1 can (14.5 oz) Muir Glen™ fire roasted diced tomatoes

1 can (4.5 oz) Old El Paso™ chopped green chiles

1 package (8 oz) cream cheese, cubed, softened

2 cups shredded sharp Cheddar cheese (8 oz)

8 oz cavatappi pasta, cooked and drained as directed on package (about 3 cups)

Chopped fresh cilantro leaves, if desired

## Steps

- 1

Spray 5-quart slow cooker with cooking spray. In slow cooker, mix enchilada sauce, taco seasoning mix and chicken until chicken is coated.

- 2

Add onion, garlic, tomatoes and green chiles to slow cooker; mix well. Cover; cook on Low heat setting 3 to 3 1/2 hours or until juice of chicken is clear when thickest part is cut (at least 165°F).

- 3

Remove chicken from slow cooker, and transfer to cutting board; let stand about 5 minutes or until cool enough to handle. Meanwhile, stir cream cheese and Cheddar cheese into slow cooker. Cover; cook on High heat setting 5 to 10 minutes or until cheese melts. Stir thoroughly to incorporate.

- 4

Meanwhile, shred chicken with 2 forks; return to slow cooker, and stir in cooked pasta. Cover; cook on High heat setting 5 to 10 minutes or until heated through. Garnish with cilantro before serving.

# *Slow-Cooker Cheesy White Chicken Lasagna*

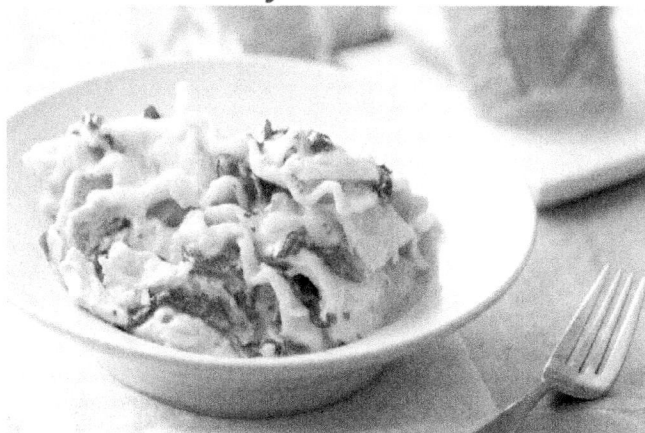

- Prep15 MIN

## Ingredients

8 oz uncooked lasagna noodles, broken into 2-inch pieces

2 cups shredded cooked chicken

1/2 cup chopped onion

2 teaspoons finely chopped garlic

1 jar (15 oz) Alfredo pasta sauce

1 1/2 cups Progresso™ chicken broth (from 32-oz carton)

1/2 teaspoon dried basil leaves

1/2 teaspoon salt

1/4 teaspoon black pepper

1 1/2 cups shredded Italian cheese blend (6 oz)

1 package (5 oz) fresh baby spinach

## Steps

- 1

Spray 4-quart slow cooker with cooking spray. Add lasagna noodles, chicken, onion, garlic, Alfredo sauce, chicken broth, basil, salt and pepper to slow cooker. Stir gently; stir in 1 cup of the cheese.

- 2

Cover and cook on Low heat setting 1 1/2 hours; stir mixture thoroughly until pasta is covered in sauce. Cover; cook 1 1/2 hours longer or until pasta is tender.

- 3

Gradually add spinach, carefully stirring to wilt; sprinkle with remaining 1/2 cup cheese. Increase to High heat setting; cover and cook 5 to 10 minutes or until cheese is melted.

# *Slow-Cooker Meatballs and Tortellini*

## Ingredients

### Meatballs

1 lb lean (at least 80%) ground beef

1 egg

3/4 cup Progresso™ Italian Bread Crumbs 15oz (89102)

1 teaspoon salt

1/4 teaspoon ground black pepper

### Sauce, Pasta and Toppings

1 can (16 oz) Muir Glen™ organic diced tomatoes, undrained

2 tablespoons canned Muir Glen™ organic tomato paste

1 cup Progresso™ chicken broth (from 32-oz carton)

1 tablespoon Italian seasoning

1 teaspoon salt

1/4 teaspoon ground black pepper

1 package (10 oz) refrigerated cheese tortellini

1/2 cup grated Parmesan cheese

Chopped fresh basil leaves, if desired

**Steps**

- 1

In large bowl, mix Meatball ingredients. Shape mixture into 12 round meatballs.

- 2

In 6-quart slow cooker, mix diced tomatoes, tomato paste, broth, Italian seasoning, 1 teaspoon salt and 1/4 teaspoon pepper. Add meatballs to slow cooker.

- 3

Cover and cook on High heat setting 3 hours or on Low heat setting 6 hours or until meatballs are completely cooked through.

- 4

Add tortellini; cover and cook 10 to 15 minutes or until soft.

- 5

Serve meatballs and tortellini with Parmesan cheese and basil.

## Slow-Cooker Spinach Alfredo Lasagna

- Prep30 MIN

## Ingredients

2 boxes (10 oz each) frozen chopped spinach

2 1/2cups shredded Italian cheese blend (10 oz)

2 jars (15 oz each) Alfredo pasta sauce

12 uncooked lasagna noodles

3 cups chopped cooked chicken

1/2 cup freshly shredded Parmesan cheese (2 oz)

1 medium tomato, diced

## Steps

- 1

Cook and drain spinach as directed on package; squeeze out as much liquid as possible. Set aside.

- 2

Spray 5-quart oval slow cooker with cooking spray.

- 3

In large bowl, mix 1 cup of the cheese blend and the Alfredo sauce.

- 4

In slow cooker, spread one-fourth of the sauce mixture. Layer with 3 of the uncooked noodles (breaking noodles as needed to fit), one-third of the chicken, one-third of the spinach and 1/2 cup of the cheese blend. Repeat layers twice. Top with remaining noodles, sauce mixture and the Parmesan cheese.

- 5

Cover; cook on Low heat setting 3 1/2 to 4 1/2 hours or until edges are bubbly and center is heated through. Let stand 10 minutes; sprinkle with diced tomato before serving.

# *Slow-Cooker Mac and Cheese*

• Prep20 MIN

## Ingredients

3 1/2 cups whole milk

1 can (12 oz) evaporated milk

1/2 cup butter, melted

1 teaspoon Dijon mustard

3/4 teaspoon salt

1/4 teaspoon black pepper

1/8 teaspoon ground red pepper (cayenne)

1 box (16 oz) elbow macaroni

4 cups shredded Cheddar cheese (16 oz)

8 oz Kraft™ Velveeta™ cheese, cut into 1/2-inch cubes

1/2 cup shredded Parmesan cheese

2 tablespoons butter

2/3 cup Progresso™ plain panko crispy bread crumbs

## Steps

- 1

Spray 5-quart slow cooker with cooking spray. In slow cooker, beat milks, melted butter, mustard, salt and peppers with whisk. Add macaroni and 3 1/2 cups of the Cheddar cheese, the cubed cheese and Parmesan cheese. Cover; cook on Low heat setting 1 hour. Stir well. Cover; cook 1 to 1 1/2 hours or until pasta is cooked, but not mushy.

- 2

Stir until mac and cheese is combined and creamy. Sprinkle remaining 1/2 cup Cheddar cheese on top. Cover; let stand about 15 minutes or until melted.

- 3

Meanwhile, in 8-inch skillet, heat 2 tablespoons butter over medium heat. Add bread crumbs; stir to coat. Cook and stir about 3 minutes or until lightly browned. Sprinkle over mac and cheese, and serve.

## *Slow-Cooker Barbecue Bacon, Chicken and Cheddar Pasta*

- 

Prep20 MIN

## Ingredients

3 cups whole milk

1 can (12 oz) evaporated milk

1/2 cup barbecue sauce

1/4 cup butter, melted

1 1/4 teaspoons salt

1/2 teaspoon black pepper

1/8 teaspoon ground red pepper (cayenne)

1 package (16 oz) uncooked penne pasta

4 cups shredded Cheddar cheese (16 oz)

8 oz Kraft™ Velveeta™ cheese, cut into 1/2-inch cubes

8 slices bacon, crisply cooked and crumbled

3 cups shredded deli rotisserie chicken

2 tablespoons butter

2/3 cup Progresso™ plain panko crispy bread crumbs

## Steps

- 1

Spray inside of 5-quart slow cooker with cooking spray. In slow cooker, beat milk, evaporated milk, 1/4 cup of the barbecue sauce, the melted butter, salt, pepper and red pepper with whisk. Add pasta, 3 1/2 cups of the Cheddar cheese and the Velveeta™ cheese. Cover; cook on Low heat setting 2 1/2 to 3 hours or until pasta is cooked, but not mushy.

- 2

Reserve 1/4 cup of the crumbled bacon.

- 3

When the pasta has cooked, increase to High heat setting; stir in chicken and remaining bacon. Sprinkle remaining 1/2 cup Cheddar cheese on top. Cover; cook about 15 minutes or until melted. Turn off slow cooker and let stand, still covered, 15 minutes.

- 4

Meanwhile, in 6-inch skillet, heat 2 tablespoons butter over medium heat. Add bread crumbs, and stir to coat. Cook and stir 3 to 4 minutes or until golden brown. Add reserved 1/4 cup bacon to bread crumbs. Sprinkle crumbs and bacon over pasta. Drizzle with remaining 1/4 cup barbecue sauce, and serve.

# Slow-Cooker Cheesy Ham and Noodles

-                Prep 15 MIN

## Ingredients

12 oz uncooked linguine

3 cups half-and-half

2 cups shredded Swiss cheese (8 oz)

1 cup frozen sweet peas (from 12-oz bag), thawed

1 tablespoon Dijon mustard

12 oz lean cooked ham steak, chopped

1 container (10 oz) refrigerated Alfredo pasta sauce

## Steps

- 1

Spray 3 1/2- to 4-quart slow cooker with cooking spray. In 4-quart saucepan, cook linguine 5 minutes in boiling water; drain. Place linguine in slow cooker. Add half-and- half, 1 cup of the cheese, the peas, mustard, ham and Alfredo sauce; stir gently to blend. Sprinkle with remaining 1 cup cheese.

- 2

Cover; cook on Low heat setting 3 hours or until linguine is tender.

# *Slow-Cooker Chicken Broccoli Lasagna*

- 

Prep 20 MIN

## Ingredients

1 1/2 cups Cascadian Farm™ Frozen Organic Broccoli Florets

3 cups chopped cooked chicken

3 1/2 cups shredded Italian cheese blend (14 oz)

3/4 teaspoon freshly ground pepper

1 can (10 3/4 oz) condensed cream of chicken soup

1 can (10 3/4 oz) condensed cream of mushroom soup

1 container (8 oz) sour cream

1 package (8 oz) sliced fresh mushrooms (about 3 cups)

9 uncooked lasagna noodles

1 cup freshly shredded Parmesan cheese (4 oz)

## Steps

- 1

Cook and drain broccoli as directed on package, using minimum cook time. In large bowl, mix chicken, 2 cups of the cheese blend, the pepper, both soups, sour cream, mushrooms and broccoli.

- 2

Spray 5-quart slow cooker with cooking spray. Spread one-fourth of the chicken mixture in slow cooker. Layer with 3 of the uncooked noodles (breaking noodles as needed to fit), one-fourth of the chicken mixture and 1/2 cup of the cheese blend. Repeat layers twice. Sprinkle with Parmesan cheese.

- 3

Cover; cook on Low heat setting 3 hours 30 minutes or until bubbly and noodles are tender. Let stand 10 minutes before serving. Sprinkle with additional freshly ground pepper, if desired.

# SLOW-COOKER PASTA RECIPES READY IN 1 ½ TO 3 HOURS

*Slow-Cooker Buffalo Chicken Rigatoni*

- Prep25 MIN

## Ingredients

8 boneless skinless chicken thighs

1/2 teaspoon celery salt

1/4 teaspoon salt

1/4 teaspoon pepper

1/3 cup Buffalo wing sauce

2 cloves garlic, finely chopped

8 oz cream cheese, softened and cubed

1 1/2 cups shredded Cheddar cheese (6 oz)

12 oz rigatoni, cooked and drained as directed on package

1/3 cup blue cheese crumbles

1/3 cup thinly sliced green onions

## Steps

- 1

Spray 5-quart slow cooker with cooking spray. Sprinkle chicken with celery salt, salt and pepper; arrange in slow cooker. Pour Buffalo sauce over chicken; stir in garlic. Cover; cook on High heat setting about 2 hours or until juice of chicken is clear when thickest part is cut (at least 165°F). Remove chicken and, using two forks, shred into bite-size pieces.

- 2

Add cream cheese and Cheddar cheese to slow cooker; stir to combine. Cover; cook 15 minutes. Beat with whisk until cheeses have melted into sauce. Add rigatoni and shredded chicken; stir to combine. Cover; cook about 5 minutes or until hot. Garnish with blue cheese and green onions.

# Slow-Cooker Cheesy Chicken Spaghetti

- Prep30 MIN

## Ingredients

1 tablespoon butter, melted

1 tablespoon Worcestershire sauce

2 teaspoons seasoned salt

3 cloves garlic, finely chopped

1 package (20 oz) boneless skinless chicken thighs

1 can (28 oz) Muir Glen™ organic fire roasted diced tomatoes, drained

1 can (18 oz) Progresso™ creamy mushroom soup

1 can (4.5 oz) Old El Paso™ chopped green chiles

1 package (8 oz) cream cheese, cubed, softened

2 cups shredded sharp Cheddar cheese (8 oz)

8 oz spaghetti, cooked and drained as directed on package

2 tablespoons chopped fresh Italian (flat-leaf) parsley leaves

## Steps

- 1

Spray 5-quart slow cooker with cooking spray. In large bowl, mix melted butter, Worcestershire sauce, seasoned salt and garlic. Add chicken; toss to coat. Pour mixture into slow cooker.

- 2

In same bowl, mix tomatoes, soup and chiles; pour over chicken.

- 3

Cover; cook on High heat setting 2 to 3 hours or on Low heat setting 3 to 4 hours or until instant-read thermometer inserted in thickest part of chicken reads at least 165°F.

- 4

Remove chicken from slow cooker, and transfer to cutting board; let stand 5 minutes or until cool enough to handle. Meanwhile, stir cream cheese and Cheddar cheese into slow cooker. Cover; cook on High heat setting 5 to 10 minutes or until cheese melts. Stir.

- 5

Meanwhile, shred chicken with 2 forks; return to slow cooker, and stir in cooked spaghetti. Top with parsley.

- 6

To make ahead and freeze: In large bowl, mix melted butter, Worcestershire sauce, seasoned salt and garlic. Add chicken; toss to coat. Pour mixture into 1-gallon resealable food-storage plastic bag. In same bowl, mix tomatoes, soup and chiles; pour over chicken in bag. Seal bag, removing as much air as possible. Lay flat, and freeze up to 3 months. Thaw completely, 8 to 24 hours, in refrigerator. Spray 5-quart slow cooker with cooking spray. Pour thawed mixture into slow cooker. Follow steps 3 through 5.

# Slow-Cooker Cheesy Chicken Spaghetti

- Prep30 MIN

## Ingredients

1 tablespoon butter, melted

1 tablespoon Worcestershire sauce

2 teaspoons seasoned salt

3 cloves garlic, finely chopped

1 package (20 oz) boneless skinless chicken thighs

1 can (28 oz) Muir Glen™ organic fire roasted diced tomatoes, drained

1 can (18 oz) Progresso™ creamy mushroom soup

1 can (4.5 oz) Old El Paso™ chopped green chiles

1 package (8 oz) cream cheese, cubed, softened

2 cups shredded sharp Cheddar cheese (8 oz)

8 oz spaghetti, cooked and drained as directed on package

2 tablespoons chopped fresh Italian (flat-leaf) parsley leaves

## Steps

- 1

Spray 5-quart slow cooker with cooking spray. In large bowl, mix melted butter, Worcestershire sauce, seasoned salt and garlic. Add chicken; toss to coat. Pour mixture into slow cooker.

- 2

In same bowl, mix tomatoes, soup and chiles; pour over chicken.

- 3

Cover; cook on High heat setting 2 to 3 hours or on Low heat setting 3 to 4 hours or until instant-read thermometer inserted in thickest part of chicken reads at least 165°F.

- 4

Remove chicken from slow cooker, and transfer to cutting board; let stand 5 minutes or until cool enough to handle. Meanwhile, stir cream cheese and Cheddar cheese into slow cooker. Cover; cook on High heat setting 5 to 10 minutes or until cheese melts. Stir.

- 5

Meanwhile, shred chicken with 2 forks; return to slow cooker, and stir in cooked spaghetti. Top with parsley.

- 6

To make ahead and freeze: In large bowl, mix melted butter, Worcestershire sauce, seasoned salt and garlic. Add chicken; toss to coat. Pour mixture into 1-gallon resealable food-storage plastic bag. In same bowl, mix tomatoes, soup and chiles; pour over chicken in bag. Seal bag, removing as much air as possible. Lay flat, and freeze up to 3 months. Thaw completely, 8 to 24 hours, in refrigerator. Spray 5-quart slow cooker with cooking spray. Pour thawed mixture into slow cooker. Follow steps 3 through 5.

# Slow-Cooker Cheesy Chicken Manicotti

•    Prep30 MIN

## Ingredients

2 cups finely chopped cooked chicken

1 container (15 oz) whole-milk ricotta cheese

1 teaspoon garlic salt

1/4 teaspoon crushed red pepper flakes

1/2 cup finely chopped fresh basil leaves

14 uncooked manicotti shells (8 oz)

1 jar (25.5 oz) Muir Glen™ organic tomato basil pasta sauce

3/4 cup water

2 cups shredded mozzarella cheese (8 oz)

## Steps

- 1

In medium bowl, mix chicken, ricotta cheese, garlic salt and red pepper flakes; stir in 1/4 cup of the basil. Spoon into quart-sized resealable food-storage plastic bag. Cut 3/4 inch tip off bag. Pipe filling into manicotti shells.

- 2

Spray 5-quart oval slow cooker with cooking spray. In medium bowl, mix pasta sauce and water. Spread about one-third of the sauce mixture in slow cooker. Place 7 of the filled manicotti shells in pasta sauce. Sprinkle with 1 cup of the mozzarella cheese. Spoon another one-third of the sauce mixture over shells. Top with remaining 7 filled manicotti shells; sprinkle with remaining 1 cup mozzarella cheese. Top with remaining one-third of sauce mixture.

- 3

Cover; cook 2 to 3 hours on High heat setting or until shells are tender. Serve with remaining 1/4 cup basil.

Printed in Great Britain
by Amazon